CONQUEST OF SELF

Philip Sayetta Jacobs was born and educated in Scotland. He is a short-story writer and a student of History and Philosophy: one of his stories was made into a television play starring Joan Crawford, "The Road to Edinburgh".

Philip Sayetta Jacobs had a successful business in England and Scotland. He then moved to New York, where he developed housing estates. He was also the owner of Philip Jacobs of London, a very selective antiques establishment on Fifth Avenue in New York; and he is now a collector of and expert on old English silver and porcelain.

He and his wife, Lucille, live in Florida and spend July and August in London.

Philip Sayetta Jacobs is also the author of the best-selling *Serenity, Don't Leave Home Without It, The Mission* and *Hess, The Camouflaged Emissary*.

CONQUEST OF SELF

Philip Sayetta Jacobs

AIDAN ELLIS

First published in the United Kingdom by Aidan Ellis Publishing,
Cobb House, Nuffield, Henley on Thames, Oxon RG9 5RT

First Edition 1993

A CIP catalogue record for this book is available from the British
Library

Filmset in 12pt Times Roman by
EMS Photosetters, Thorpe Bay, Essex SS1 3JY
Printed in England by Professional Book Supplies Ltd,
Abingdon, Oxford OX13 6RX

ISBN: 0 85628 252 9

*To my wife, Lucille, and
to her positiveness.
This book is affectionately
dedicated to both*

CONQUEST OF SELF

THE MORE WE KNOW OF OUR
PASSIONS, THE LESS THEY CON-
TROL US; AND NOTHING WILL
PROTECT US FROM EXTERNAL
COMPULSION SO MUCH AS THE
CONTROL OF OURSELVES.

SCHOPENHAUER

CONTENTS

Introduction   11

1   Discover Who You Are and What You
    Can Be   17

2   How to Set Your Goals and Attain Them   29

3   There is More Logical Reason for
    Optimism than Pessimism   45

4   Slow Down and Achieve Rapid Success   61

5   What You Can Conceive You Can
    Achieve Through Intuition   73

6   Faith Without Religion   87

7   Growing Old is a Bad Habit   105

8   Success Without Stress   119

9   Take Control of Your Life   131

Introduction

Circumstances only have the power over us that we allow them to have; if we are victims, it is with our own knowledge. We can establish a sense of control over our lives by realizing that we alone are responsible for our own choices and actions at every level. How to live was of paramount importance to the ancient philosophers, who knew that life with a purpose was superior to a pleasure-seeking alternative.

The theme of this book, I must state clearly from the outset, is that our greatest possession is complete possession of ourselves. From my observation, there is no happiness to compare with that gained from exercising a constant awareness of our faculties; together with maintaining access to our capabilities by vigilantly preventing our minds from losing their alertness, and avoiding becoming involuntary victims of insignificant events which carry us along.

We live in exciting but dangerous times. If we wish to survive successfully, we will need the self-mastery that comes from a permanent stability of conduct, and a method of behaviour to enable us to derive the most out of our lives.

When our minds are induced into a state of optimistic expectation by acquiring new meaningful interests, more vitality is released into our consciousness. The more these energies are released, the more deeply satisfying our lives become.

It is with such experience that this book is concerned. It explores the ways in which we may be wasting our energies, and suggests how to retain them and use them to create the quality of life we want for ourselves, when the constant state of our minds perceive objective reality at all times.

Nothing is more dull than to live life aimlessly. Nothing is more exhilarating than when the mind is most actively directing energy and attention towards additional interests. We know there is something better than ourselves within our grasp and that the possibilities are endless, but we may not know how to find it. Meaningful interests give us the ability to focus clearly on an objective and then to achieve it effortlessly. If these interests are productive, they will direct us to a better way of life than the usual cycle of day-to-day routine escapes from boredom.

Diversifications are necessary in our lives, and those who seek them acquire a poise and self-reliance which stimulate more than sufficient energy for their necessary every-day activities. It is in the moments when the mind is most active that life becomes genuinely interesting and the most intense pleasures are experienced. Those who have a wide range of interests obviously have a distinct advantage over those who have few. Our main problem is a tendency to be confined to the trivialities of our personal preoccupations and to ignore a better life of broader significance.

It is necessary to plan in order to release our hidden energies and bring potency to areas of our lives which are not satisfactory. Everyone has a mental vision of how they can improve themselves, but not everyone takes the necessary steps to turn the vision into a reality. The paradox is that, although we already possess the knowledge, we are continually postponing the effort to some time in the future instead of grasping the basic problem and deciding to remedy it now.

A sure way to prepare for the future is to make the best of the present. The more you will it, the more your mind will feed on that positiveness.

HE IS MOST POWERFUL, WHO
HAS POWER OVER HIMSELF.
                    SENECA

Philip Sayetta Jacobs
1993

Discover Who You Are and
What You Can Be

1

As the world becomes more complex and competitive, developing a self-assurance has become a more important basic necessity than it ever was in the past. In order to survive, we are going to have to learn how to adjust to constantly changing conditions, and fully understand the world in which we live. Life is incomplete without a constant possession of our faculties.

Rapid changes have created more obstacles to our psychological development than ever before. It is important to understand that, in order to improve our performance at work, or enjoy our leisure and relationship with others, we have to perfect our ability to behave effectively at all times. Although self-assurance will provide a sense of security, it does not necessarily mean we are protected from the consequences of every problem; but it does guarantee that our susceptibility to problems will be reduced and is indispensable to improving our chances of coping with anxieties, fears or any of life's difficulties. **To experience the real meaning of life is to secure the ability to be in possession of all our powers at all times.**

Many of us are dissatisfied with our lives, but do not realize the causes of the dissatisfaction. We know we are being deprived of a more satisfactory life which we believe is in our reach, but we cannot understand why others are the fortunate possessors of it.

The real problem is that our misconception of ourselves then becomes a reality. We should stop limiting ourselves to behaving in accordance with the beliefs we have in our ability. We are what we habitually think. If we acquire confidence we can accomplish our wishes and be less self doubting. We then would discover opportunities to make our expectations become a reality, taking advantage of every chance for success pursuing our ambitions.

Fear of failure is the primary reason we don't set challenging goals for ourselves. Simply, if we change our beliefs and concentrate on meaningful plans, adhering to them at all times, this will change our whole future. A consistent purpose is an indispensable condition for building the circumstances for the life we secretly desire. A determined attitude must be sustained until our goals are reached. If we don't have this, our future will be merely a replica of our past.

If we have faith in our ability to set ourselves reasonable goals, we succeed more easily. We can always make things better than they are, all we have to do is focus our attention on obtaining our expectations. **We must live with a purpose, setting goals and searching for opportunities to achieve them, rather than hoping merely for chance to change the circumstances of our lives.**

Negativity can be a major obstacle to success as it destroys our ability to exercise our faculties. However, we must not confuse goals with dreams. Goals to which we are firmly committed give us a direction to build the future we want and can change dull and confused lives into a well-balanced machine. Dreams will remain as mere fantasies if we fail to have a planned method to achieve them; or even with a well planned goal, we will lose the most essential ingredient to realizing success if we do not maintain a continuity of purpose, by perceiving our objective at all times and staying on course until we reach our target. **A determined attitude has to be maintained until our goals are reached.**

The main problem with some people is a tendency to become confined to the trivialities and monotony of their personal preoccupations. In many cases they become a helpless victim of events, which carry them along and which they regard as normal conventional occurrences. They live monotonous days and have a routine habit-formed existence, to which they attach far more importance than it deserves. Their thoughts are directed towards immediate pleasures rather than some satisfying achievement.

They may not be aware that there are many significant interests available, the pursuit of which we are all potentially capable and which will bring more meaning to our lives and will be an immense source of happiness. The more things we are interested in, the more frequently will opportunities appear to increase our happiness, and the less we will fear from being in a state of boredom. As life becomes more interesting, confidence and motivation are increased. **Those who have many interests are far superior to those who have none.**

Each one of us has a life force within us, an

untapped potential waiting to be used. Most of us are aware of it, but fail to put it into practice. We will not be restricted by boundaries or limitations, if we decide to utilize our creative skills and talents. The only limitations on what we can accomplish are those which we impose on ourselves. **There can be no great success without a great commitment.**

We all derive even further satisfaction through knowing we have successfully mastered our new interests. These will increase our worth and are certainly more fulfilling than the accumulation of possessions by those who already have more than sufficient for all possible needs.

Happiness and success are available to everyone who is willing to train the mind to be in complete possession of its faculties. All human beings possess creative powers. To fulfil their potential it is simply a matter of disgarding habits formed in our early years and carefully developing new ones by promoting a positive consciousness. This is explained in one of the following chapters on intuition.

Continuation of an unproductive everydayness will only result in a repetition of a routine with a lack of purpose. Deprived of a purpose, our minds disintegrate; with a purpose, we can analyse and take advantage of every experience. **Interesting people are usually those who are interested in everything.** Their minds can be compared with a searchlight, continually seeking new interests on which to expend their energies. Those who are dull and are devoid of interests generally seek the company of people with similar traits and the same modes of communication.

We fall into a habitual way of life, our daily activities afford very little variety; we begin to do everything unconsciously, and fail to use opportunities to be alert to the benefit of our subconscious mind. Without using the mind, what we see and experience is difficult to retain because we learn it improperly. Our inner self is just as predictable as our outer life. It never occurs to most people to try to control their minds as they do not consider this an acquisition of knowledge. By practising a mode of mind training, you will acquire an excellent method of resisting old negative habits and replacing them with new interests.

By further developing our minds, we will see into our essential nature and understand the process of finding what we really want out of our lives. With new motivations and goals, our previously undisciplined minds will automatically produce insights for their completion. In an emergency an unusual effort has to be made to stimulate us and overcome our natural laziness. With motivation and a fresh purpose you will suddenly find yourself enjoying life intensely. A state of inner peace and confidence comes after effort of this kind.

Having acquired a new and more significant mode of behaviour, you will have discovered a simple method of releasing your hidden energies for your immediate improvement. This is a characteristic usually adopted by ambitious people. You will be putting more energies into your consciousness and you will reach a state of expectant optimism. This new wide-awakeness and intenseness will make your life more interesting. Your days will cease to be monotonous and repetitious and, because of your new interests, anticipating each day with a fresh incentive will come naturally to you. You will realize you possess the ability to focus clearly on an objective and to succeed in attaining it with the least possible energy, which is the most economical way.

The purpose of this book is to resist mental laziness and negative tendencies by encouraging the practice of removing haste, the hurry and pressures from our lives and supplanting them with a positive calm and patience. If we don't, we will have no valid reason for living.

The basic key to happiness is for a person, having secured sufficient income for security, to improve the mind and inner self. This in turn generally will also increase the chances for further financial improvement, as happiness will create a positive future.

The ultimate result of activities which utilize our abilities is a new source of self-esteem and a resolve never to return to our previous way of living. Habits formed in early years are not likely to persist as we find more opportunities to develop new skills, and we can ensure that the future will not be a repetition of our past. There is nothing deep or complex about this.

Some people have a habit-formed existence, indulging in one futile activity after another, which could be because of a subconscious desire to escape the emptiness of their circumstances. They do things in haphazard sequence, not realizing that it would be more beneficial to make better use of their experiences by concentrating clearly and carefully developing an objective. This would broaden their life and help them to take responsibility for their own future, especially if they have formed a pattern of behaving in a relaxed manner. This is a necessary rhythm in our lives, if we wish to cultivate poise and self-reliance. **And if we learn to concentrate and control our minds, we can achieve harmony.**

The mind is a complex machine; many people are a bundle of impulses and emotions and only by self-analysis can they prevent a negative outcome. Any unusual effort, such as a planned goal will have the effect of stimulating the mind to become more awake, and increasing the energy flowing through the body, which will ensure that all your thinking towards achieving your objective will be clear and intense.

If up to now, you have been bored or confused and living in a negative withdrawn mental state, you can train your mind to become a well balanced machine, too busy to occupy itself with unproductive trivialities. With perseverance, you will be wholly absorbed in the work to be done. The greater the ambition, the greater the stimulation and a heightened sense of anticipation as you concentrate on its fulfilment. The moment you change your aimless way of living and become involved in a genuine quest for self-improvement, you will discover that happy people are those who face life with a feeling of security and

Discover Who You Are and What You Can Be

who have learned to conquer themselves.
An unexamined life is not worth living.

THE MORE WE KNOW OF OUR
PASSIONS, THE LESS THEY WILL
CONTROL US; AND NOTHING
WILL PROTECT US FROM EXTER-
NAL COMPULSION SO MUCH AS
THE CONTROL OF OURSELVES.

SCHOPENHAUER

How to Set Your Goals and Attain Them

2

There is increasing evidence that our minds contain more resources than we had ever believed possible. During the course of our lives, we actually use only a small percentage of our total brain capacity; but there is a genuine possibility that there is something we can comfortably do to utilize more of it. If we take the time to understand ourselves, we can use our brains more effectively. Most of the thoughts that crowd our minds are persistently useless. Many of us have unfortunate behaviour patterns, which are the result of poor thinking and which work to our disadvantage. Only when we consciously act in a planned direction do we narrow our concentration to our particular task, which is most important. **As long as our minds remain untrained and our thoughts are unrestricted, we cannot succeed in attaining our goals.**

We all plan to improve our business or personal life and we do succeed in achieving the results we want some of the time, but unfortunately few of us are able to maintain these results consistently. We experience difficulty in making our changes permanent. We know how to awaken our enthusiasm, but do not know how to sustain it. We remember dimly that we had a vision, but unfortunately we repeatedly return to our old habits. Continuity of purpose is the essential ingredient for attaining and maintaining our success.

Altering our beliefs and reappraising our way of life is useless unless we develop a permanent method of sustaining that change. If we don't, we are losing an opportunity to improve ourselves. The brain is a dynamic organ, it is entirely possible to alter our old negative habits through it. If you choose to develop new abilities, your brain, like any other organ, will develop more as you exercise it. We know what to do, but do we do what we know? If we are really determined, we could at any moment overcome weakness by resolving now that our minds will cease to be open to profitless thoughts by giving them a decisive turn in a chosen direction every time they stray. Before we attempt to accomplish anything, we must not only believe it possible, but be prepared to utilize most of our capabilities in its pursuit, realizing that it is of paramount importance to take heed of what thoughts we entertain. Entertaining wrong thoughts is not very different from entertaining wrong company; both contribute to a waste of energy. **Efficiency can be increased by the cultivation of an orderly mind which focuses on matters adequately at the appropriate time, rather than inadequately at all times.**

If the mind habitually rejects insignificant thoughts, attentiveness to the important ones will increase. Cultivating the will to master our abilities is a necessary part of the process, otherwise we are merely setting ourselves up for failure. **Ultimately, all success will come from within.** If you are enthusiastic, disciplined and possess set beliefs and strategies, you will eventually be rewarded. If results are unsatisfactory, then your new concentration has no merit, as obviously you have succumbed to your old spontaneous habits.

Only by removing negative thoughts will confidence return. If you are avoiding a particular task, you may be sending yourself unrealistic negative messages. By concentrating your attention you can positively boost your motivation: we have a tendency to discount our accomplishments and focus on what we are unable to do.

You should have a picture in your mind of what you want yourself to be; everything comes to those who wait. As Plato said, "The world belongs to the patient man." A human being with a carefully planned goal and a developed method of behaviour, using the best of his abilities, must accomplish his desires. Nothing will resist a will that will stay on course until the goals are realized. A strong motive will keep you intensely alive and awaken powerful creative possibilities, and the rewards of a consistent purpose are innumerable.

A dedicated, strongly developed purpose is an indispensable condition and the most important ingredient of triumphing over adverse circumstances. We cannot expect to succeed in our aims if we live from one detached episode to another, as the absence of a prearranged plan means we are drifting without direction. Many people have not formed an overall plan for their lives, they do everything piecemeal and it is only by chance that they achieve anything. They drift with their circumstances and believe they have an ambition, which they probably do half-heartedly, but they lack the effort needed for its realization.

Success will escape you unless you prepare the circumstances for its development; as, even if you are potentially capable, your old habit-filled routine in which you gave priority to insignificant matters will continue to reappear. The energy wasted on trivialities could be used more wisely if properly directed.

A practical proven technique for achieving your goals is to visualize everything you crave. Let us take a period of the next twelve months; accomplishments are easier in stages and in order to prevent stress one year is a conveniently allotted time for each stage. You cannot focus on the entire task in front of you, it has to be taken one step at a time, and several steps or stages will eventually enable you to reach your final objective. **A great part of stress is caused by the desperation to achieve ambitions in the shortest time possible.**

Maintain an image in your mind of exactly what you expect to achieve in the next year, keep it constantly with you as you would a jigsaw puzzle when you are actively engaged in locating the missing pieces necessary for its completion. The achievement of your aims is similar to the completion of the puzzle. During the time you have allotted for its fulfillment, you must continually retain the picture of the desired objective in your mind. Picture yourself adopting the specific behaviour pattern you want in your life and focus on the image of your desires to the exclusion of everything else. Sooner or later your mind will become receptive after sustained concentration and, being alert for opportunities, you will have hunches which fill in the missing pieces, usually when you least expect them.

If you have not set your mind's image towards a realistic goal or fail to maintain it, you will miss the opportunity of filling in these pieces when they appear. We should all learn how to benefit from our subconscious mind, with its unlimited storehouse of knowledge and past experiences. As I will describe in one of the following chapters, your subconscious mind will have an enormous influence in helping you find the missing pieces to your jigsaw puzzle. There is nothing complicated about this technique; as you become more proficient, you will find that the pieces will appear more often. You will find that this mind picture will be very effective in inducing a condition of mental concentration and you will cease to view things negatively, as your mind will become a well-balanced, orderly machine, too busy to be occupied with matters that are not important to your goals.

The image in your mind of what you are aiming for will produce a positive alertness, assisting you to generate the self motivation you need to keep your ambitions alive, and directing your mind to their possession. You will be well aware that you have mastered the technique when your mind's attention ceases to wander. What we have to fear is a natural tendency to become discouraged when we question the success of the technique, as our pessimism could result in a dissipation of our energy and confidence. If you are really determined, you cannot fail, you are never a failure until you give up. Simply make a strong, clear resolution that the picture in your mind will eventually exist as an accomplished fact. When it does, and you have completed the last piece of the jigsaw, prepare a new picture for new goals, an extension of your old one for the coming year. **Success will make you regard time as a precious possession and you will no longer throw it away thoughtlessly.**

If your goals are achieved sooner than expected, or if you find the present aims are not motivating or stimulating you sufficiently, in these cases, it is simply a matter of forming new ambitions or revising your present ones.

Setting intelligent targets is a true essence of self-direction, recognizing our needs becomes easier if we are clear what they are. We must not lose touch with our real needs and substitute those we are conditioned to believe we should have. We must know where we are going and choose our goals carefully; otherwise, we are likely to mistake confused activity for accomplishment. What is the use of being overly busy if we have no set purpose? When you picture yourself in your mind, you see yourself as the person you might become if you are able to alter your circumstances. You will see that life can be infinitely meaningful and nothing in this world could be more important than maintaining that meaning.

Whatever your goals are, financial or otherwise, be sure that the aims for which you are striving honestly reflect the things you desire most and which are of prime importance to yourself, not those you believe others would expect of you. **You cannot measure achievements in terms of praise by others,** and if you do, you will be doomed to frustration as the targets you set must be for yourself alone. You must have an outlook on life that ignores the generally accepted philosophy that life is a contest in which respect is only accorded to the winner. Pursuing goals will not produce satisfaction, nor will you reap any advantage from your achievements, if your only purpose for achieving success is entirely to receive other people's admiration. You will fail to achieve satisfaction and fulfilment from the goals you have chosen, if you cannot distinguish between the ones set for yourself and those set to impress others.

If people, whose intelligence and background are entirely different from yours, are chosen by you as judges of your new success, this could be an obstacle to your happiness. The personal satisfaction you will receive from your achievements should definitely supersede the pride of displaying them, and in the end, you will be much more respected. We must avoid the tendency to fashion our ambitions to conform to the imagined expectations or applause of those around us. Any attempt to improve our circumstances is more likely to succeed if the purpose of that attempt is for our own personal satisfaction and not dependent on outside approval. If our rewards are only to be measured by the encouragement of those we know, then they are too dearly earned and we are less likely to succeed.

You should confirm that what you are doing corresponds to your mind picture and at times review the progress you are making. You have to expect, as you go along, some of your ambitions ceasing to be important; and in that case, you should modify them to reflect the changes and revise your goals. Getting your priorities right is an important step of the procedure. Time spent on insignificant matters means less time for those which are important to you. You must have a clear vision of what you really want, and understand that succeeding in your aims will take longer if you are hurried. Being full of haste and pressures will postpone their achievement. One of the following chapters in this book will expose the danger of hurrying as an obstacle to self-confidence. If you reduce your pace and take life deliberately slowly, your emotional responses will be modified and you will acquire a calm and patience, which will help you function more creatively. Your mind will be alert and will be receptive to important hunches for solving and improving your plans or any other specific problems.

If you are determined to apply energy and faith and ignore discouraging tendencies, you cannot fail.

As long as your mind remains untrained and your thoughts move unrestricted with no aim in view, you will never be sensitive to the true significance of your life. The consequence of observing your own thoughts, and becoming fully aware of their origin, are measurably important, for when you acquire confidence in the possible results, the fruits of success will show themselves in your character. You will find that inspirations will automatically begin to appear, your sense of awareness will be heightened and you will notice a definite increase in your vitality. Your outlook on life will become wider and you will have a greater zest for living; and a source of power and knowledge which previously may have been neglected or untapped will be revealed as a source of strength and guidance. This will lead to a new reception of intuitive knowledge, which will envelop your entire personality, and even if you have not yet reached your goals, your efforts will be well compensated by your mental gain.

Sustained faith in your objectives will certainly move you in the right direction and will prevent you from any negative influence which can dissipate your energy or confidence. Refrain from discussing your aims with friends who may be anxious to share their pessimism with you; they could instil doubt on your own abilities and encourage your fear of failure. All you would be doing is rehearsing your own defeat by anticipating obstacles. When you lose confidence, you give up more easily, fail more often, and aspire to less.

It would be unrealistic to assume that successful people achieve their goals without frustrations and doubts. They also encounter obstacles, but are not unduly disheartened by disappointments and persevere until they are eliminated. Their ability to overcome problems is a key ingredient to their success; they treat their problems like challenges, concentrating on the advantages and rejecting the disadvantages. You will not be successful in making your dreams come true until you have learned to persevere in the face of obstacles. Disappointments very often precede success, the failure is not learning from them. **People generally make two mistakes at the same time, the first is the mistake itself, the second is not to correct it.** If your failures are caused by a weakness in your character, you can take steps to eliminate the weakness. Or, if they are due to a handicap, you have to try not to be overwhelmed by it.

Nothing in the world can replace persistence, not even talent. Many unsuccessful people are talented and educated. This world is full of educated derelicts. All human beings possess the power of persistence, it is simply a matter of developing this power by remaining in a state of continual awareness, with a goal in front and not behind us. In the recesses of our being, we can find peace and wisdom only if we exercise control over thoughts.

IT IS NOT AN EASY THING FOR A PRINCIPLE TO BECOME A MAN'S OWN, UNLESS EACH DAY HE MAINTAINS IT.

EPICTETUS

There is More Logical Reason for
Optimism than Pessimism

3

Logically, it pays to be an optimist, especially when those around you are pessimists. Only by the interest and experience we derive from them do events become satisfying. Without this satisfaction we lose our sense of proportion and miss opportunities for making life worth living.

Perhaps the best way to define the difference between an optimist and a pessimist is simply the difference between success and failure. Pessimists generally are indifferent to their day-to-day existence, nothing is done purposefully, their only indulgence being a negative desire to escape their listlessness and boredom. They lack interest as they make no attempt to change their circumstances and, therefore, tend to drift aimlessly, moving from one futile activity to another. They are afraid of solitude, believing it will inevitably lead to an intolerable ache when they are alone. They have no outline of or any preplanned structure for their future, believing their negativity to have been acquired by logical reasoning. They have an image of themselves perpetually incurring their own failure and behave as if they enjoy that outlook.

This is due to a mistaken attitude to life, and is a result of a series of undirected habits, which have destroyed a natural outlook for anything positive as they become more and more accustomed to their way of life and their inability to become interested in anything which is not failure oriented. This finally becomes part of their character. They may even be cynical towards optimists who anticipate many meaningful experiences in all their activities and who view adverse circumstances as temporary setbacks, which they minimize as much as possible.

Optimists radiate enthusiasm as they identify hope as a powerful force, which can develop their well being and lead to success; in contrast to the scepticism of pessimists, who do not realize that the absence of a goal in their life has eliminated an essential ingredient to happiness, and may result in a feeling of hopelessness. The optimist is on the lookout for favourable opportunities, and is much better adapted to this world as he maintains a vigorous enthusiasm for whatever project has his interest. He knows the solution of most everyday problems lies within the power of each individual who, with the average good fortune, can achieve most of his desires. **All that is required is to cultivate the skill of learned optimism.**

Positiveness induces a feeling of security, which enables us to confront every situation in life with confidence. It will produce a power of mastery, which will sustain us continuously in the most difficult circumstances.

An optimist is superior to a pessimist as he possesses many psychological ingredients, which produce a highly creative state. He thinks in positive terms, gets positive results and generally succeeds. He has acquired a sense of personal control which has increased his self-esteem and is, therefore, generally interested in as many things as necessary to occupy his time. He accepts life cheerfully, in contrast to the pessimist, who does not purposely plan his time and merely drifts, leaving his life to the chance of fate.

Despair of the future is rare in the mind of an optimist, who will have a completely different outlook, having sought a valid reason for living, and maintaining a buoyant expectation towards a definite sense of purpose. A positive attitude is more likely to produce an orderly method of working with less chance of experiencing mental fatigue, as confidence in achieving objectives stimulates the employment of all the optimist's skills. The more often optimists succeed, the more energy they put into their tasks and this in turn increases their success and energy, as both feed on each other. As they are constantly alert for opportunities, their positiveness is maintained each day, which frequently helps them to succeed in achieving results. They find a meaning in everything they do in terms of their ultimate goal, even the little things.

Positiveness and persistence are more necessary for success than talent or education. When we are motivated by a driving force, we are kept alert as to what are the things we really most desire and, therefore, are more disciplined in proceeding to gradually acquire them. You can choose your attitude at any given moment and if you choose optimism, you will enhance your brain power, for you pour more energy into whatever you are doing when in a state of optimistic expectation. Being wholly absorbed in attaining the things you desire will prove to be effective in inducing a condition of mental concentration which will overcome the weakness of reacting negatively. **It is a simple formula: if you concentrate on expecting positive results, you will in most cases succeed.**

On the contrary, if your mind is conditioned to think negatively, you will ultimately acquire a tendency towards seeking your expectations. Optimism, if practised piecemeal, will fail as you will have a habit of giving up easily. It must be maintained steadfastly with constant vigilance. This is indispensable to its success. In the beginning, you look for improvement, later you plan for perfection, and when you find it, your life will take on a new significance.

A positive attitude can be a potent weapon against illness. Optimists enjoy better health, age much better and may perhaps lengthen their life. Just as they habitually overcome negative situations, they overcome bad health by positive health visualizations. People with a higher immune activity are generally positive thinkers; and conversely, negative thinkers suffer the effects of their pessimism in the chemistry of their body, as negativeness can be a source of exhaustion if all they are doing is preparing themselves for defeat. However, positiveness will increase our vitality and zest as it produces a disciplined appraisal of situations. Complicated issues are now approached simply, and curable forms of ill health are warded off as increased energy, resulting from optimism, is sufficient to deter illness and maintain good health. **Optimists retain their ambitions, despite handicaps, as they adopt a positiveness in all situations.**

Pessimists constantly anticipate misfortune. And as this is generally a lifelong ingrained habit they make no attempt to cope with it. Being wholly absorbed in their expectations, they may even promote misfortune, always assuming that it is around the corner and believe their circumstances are a series of events beyond their control.

Unless pessimists succeed in breaking this hold on their habitual thinking, they can become a victim of fatigue, as they are always overcome by what they consider is inevitable. Their way of life and outlook on the world is unacceptable to the optimist who knows there is no better pursuit for a man than to direct himself to a purpose and proceed to fulfil that purpose. Pessimists endure unnecessary pain throughout their life and are uncomfortable in the company of people who have positive interests. If they examined their feelings, they would see that their frustrations are caused by themselves and not by outside influences.

Some people have so formed the habit of expecting the worst that they are willing to suffer in advance for what they believe fate has in store for them, and become anxious to get the expected adverse news over with. They genuinely believe something negative is going to occur anyway, and are satisfied if the bad news is not as bad as they feared. They strive for pain to the exclusion of pleasure and are preoccupied with events which have not yet occurred instead of taking effective action to overcome their self-defeating behaviour.

It sounds ridiculous, but they have been unable to cure themselves of permitting their pessimism to torment them. Without making an effort to understand that they have conditioned themselves to see things in an unproductive way they fail to make a positive interpretation of what is actually happening. The only way to escape the tyranny of pessimism is to acquire wide-ranging interests. **Both good and bad habits are formed the same way, through repetition.** By understanding this simple function we can change any negative habit to a positive one. A simple step by itself, it will immediately produce positive results. One conscious act, together with an enthusiasm for some new project, will have the desired effect and is a necessary beginning to examining a new approach to life. When the right spirit is present, the power generated is incredible, new ideas will appear and everything will soon fall in line. **Each of us has the choice to think and act either positively or negatively**, it is an option between harmony and frustration. If you choose the negative, all you are doing is encouraging yourself to have a miserable life. Even if you have a positive plan which exceeds your capabilities, at least you will be stimulated to achieve most of your desires, as you will be stressing the positive elements of your personality and qualifications.

There is no greater obstacle to sound judgement than pessimism. A mind filled with worries, fears, and other disturbances is in no fit condition to solve problems, as these are an obstacle to correct thinking. When our minds are absorbed with negativeness, we are not likely to make correct decisions, as we are closed to productive solutions and merely anticipate when and in what form failure will appear.

Generally, good news is accepted as a temporary good fortune by pessimists with the expectation that, as one worry disappears, a new one will appear to replace it. On the other hand, optimists are not frustrated by failures; they see them as temporary setbacks, having acquired sufficient confidence in their own problem-solving, to know that matters will automatically right themselves. They understand that defeats are caused either by circumstances or by their own bad judgement and, as a result, they quickly recover from them. As I have already said, they have learned that people generally make two mistakes at the same time, the first is the mistake itself, the second is not to correct it.

Optimism is self-affirming; once you reap its benefits, you will devote your efforts to practising the discipline and which will offer you the opportunity of discovering a new life that previously may have not been too productive. Optimism will uncover a source of power and knowledge which has been dormant and motivate you in establishing abilities and skills which have been neglected or untapped. You can open a door to your real self and give yourself a valid reason for living merely by changing your way of thinking. If you do, your mind will be directed to your full potential, constantly alert to the possibilities of opportunities and new ideas, which will now attract themselves to you like a magnet.

Successful people impose a discipline on themselves by visualizing a goal in their mind and being convinced they will eventually achieve it. Positiveness guarantees opportunities for ambition, as it is an essential ingredient of accomplishing your desires. If you go through life with an insecure outlook, you will lose your zest and miss out on success. Optimism enhances your mental ability, and by choosing to become an optimist you have already taken an important first step. Your brain has certain computer-like qualities and, when you decide to do something new, you are creating a program for a new activity. Once your mind has new ideas, it will follow up on them.

Fear of failure is the most common pitfall to success. However, you are never a failure until you give up, as success often appears disguised as failure. Success is assumed to be the result of good judgement, good judgement is considered to be the result of experience, yet experience is usually the result of bad judgements, as we learn more from our mistakes than our achievements. We can therefore assume that those who are successful became successful because they failed more often than others. The biggest confidence builder is learning to handle failures; if you are afraid of mistakes, you will avoid accomplishing anything. Without failure, there is no growth; only by knowing what does not work, will we know what will work. People who lack the courage to fail, also lack what it takes to become an achiever. Accepting failure builds strength and wisdom, every failure is a step towards success. Learning from others who overcame failure is a good lesson and creates a resilience in us and enables us to bounce back.

It takes a lot of guts to persist in the face of rejection, to keep going in the face of defeat and to ignore the criticism of others. A firm belief in your own talents is often the difference between achieving success or merely talking about what you will accompish one day. A man who won't give up until he realizes his goal is setting himself up for success. He analyses his circumstances, maximizes the advantages and approaches the situation with confidence that he will succeed. It is perserverance, which in reality is a positive stubbornness, that helps fight weakness and makes one hold on until things get better. Optimists do everything they can to improve their situation, they put their energy into examining what exactly an adverse situation means to them. What is so dreadful or anxiety producing about it? They focus their attention on whatever catastrophic situations they are imagining and put them into a proper prospective. If their perspective is unrealistic, they modify it. Everything passes, and when it does, it leaves you stronger as a result of your positive attitude.

If we wish to conquer ourselves, we will have to confront our fears and prevent them from taking control of our thinking and dissipating our energies. We must avoid being perpetually hampered by matters which will probably never happen, and which inhibit us from being ourselves. Only when we have learned that living itself produces a certain amount of insecurity and we cannot spend our whole life resisting, will we experience life to the full. Positiveness will help overcome or avoid obstacles as it teaches us to become wholly receptive to each moment. We all experience life's inevitable problems or setbacks, but each of us approaches them differently. Optimists are much more likely to take chances as they have a record of frequently succeeding; in contrast to pessimists who put less effort into whatever they are doing and are more prone to failure.

However, as there are exceptions to every rule, we must weigh the consequences of our every action. In a situation where the possibility of failure would be disastrous, pessimism should take priority over optimism and you would be advised in this instance to take the negative approach. Pessimism can be necessary as you have to be aware of the dangers of failure. If a man is thinking of placing all his money on a roulette table, then his only safeguard is pessimism. Optimism, like everything else, should be flexible. You cannot ignore the possibilities of failure in important matters, and must take into account any negative aspect.

A man with adequate health and zest will overcome all misfortune by emerging wiser after each setback, refusing to allow one or several failures to alter his positiveness. If your character is such that you can be defeated by one failure, then you were already defeated before you started.

ONLY KNOWLEDGE AND FREE-
DOM IS POWER AND THE ONLY
PERMANENT HAPPINESS IS THE
PURSUIT OF KNOWLEDGE AND
THE JOY OF UNDERSTANDING.

SPINOZA

Slow Down and Achieve Rapid Success

4

Many people live at such a hectic pace that they lose their sense of proportion; they are driven by emotions and not by reason and have no concept of their true desires. Successful living is impossible without having control of yourself, and **only by slowing your pace can you gain a constant control of what is going on around you.** It is so simple that people are hesitant to practise it. If you do, you will accomplish much more with less effort, in less time, and be less likely to make mistakes. Adopting a deliberately slow pace will provide the opportunity to satisfactorily utilize the best of your capabilities in whatever you are doing and then, having succeeded, go on to your next assignment without supposing you could have done it better if you had had more time.

Making hurried decisions can be a strain. Time is precious and can be used wisely merely by eliminating haste from your daily life. The moment you do, you will see the benefits. Slowing down will make you more sensitive to your schedules; if you find they are excessive, they can be diminished by gradually reducing the time spent on less important activities, thus avoiding being overcome by their pressures. When you reduce your pace, your work will become more efficient and will be sustained for longer periods without your experiencing tiredness, or nervous fatigue; and you will find yourself increasingly able to resist temptations to which you have previously succumbed. It will also prevent you from occupying your mind with trivial matters when there are more immediate, significant ones which need attention. With your new pace, it will be easy to determine which matters are truly important and deserve priority and those which can be delayed until later. ✓

You can comfortably attend to those that are important and part of your main objective, if you are not wasting time and energy on ones which are not. Generally, those who are in a constant rush deliberately choose to deal with unimportant matters first, as these require less thinking ability, in preference to the important ones which require a considerable slowing down to develop a state of thinking creatively for their solutions. When you are relaxed, creative and intellectual problems will work themselves out without effort, as the tensions in you die down and your mind is in a state of clear awareness. If errors are committed, your new behaviour pattern will give you ample time to examine the causes.

If you do not shirk from the effort of living life more slowly you will retain a calmness and resist the feeling that everything must be attended to immediately. Our behaviour styles influence the way we react to events in our personal and business activities, therefore the time we give to each matter can make a significant difference to our work schedule. We can attribute most of our difficulties to performing our daily chores in high gear and not learning to use our energy wisely. We expend ourselves unncessarily, which is not only tiring, but can eventually exhaust us. Hurry will affect your thinking and your perspective of what you are doing, as it is a negative time waster, and the root cause of improper planning. People who fail in business have often found that the lack of a calm patience was the cause. Some people are not aware that their most precious possession is being constantly in control of themselves and their thoughts. They do not give themselves time to think of what they might have done differently if they had taken more time to analyse their goals clearly.

How often do you hear others complain that they just don't have sufficient time for anything. We hear this from those who are constantly busy with insignificant day-to-day activities. If they were properly organized they would not complain of insufficient time, as they would know what they had to do and allotted the proper time for the completion of each task. We would not be taken by surprise when the unexpected happens, if we anticipate distractions and not allow them to disturb us. **We should cultivate the art of thinking creatively and determining our real interests by seeing into and realizing our essential nature.** This will permeate our entire being with a new mental gain, which can only be accomplished when we change pace and slow down.

Truthfully, we are never really short of time as we all have the same twenty-four hours each day. If we

find we do not have sufficient time, it is merely
evidence of a lack of an effective purpose in dealing
with it. Hurry deters us from viewing past decisions
productively, and stops us from being aware whether
our goals and efforts really relate to our best
interests. The regularly repeated practice of doing
everything slowly will have the effect of removing the
pressures and the restlessness with which we are
afflicted, replacing them with a calm and patience
and an improved thinking ability.

Hurry is a deterrent to self-improvement, and is an
obstacle to exercising our faculties to the full when
difficult decisions have to be made, as it prevents us
maintaining the perspective of our ultimate objective.
All we produce when we do things quickly is a great
deal of stress. Only the absence of hurry can cultivate
a quiet self-confidence, which will allow us to
develop harmoniously, enabling us to complete
twice as much work in half the time. With a steady
pace, you will learn to control your mind. It never
occurs to most people to try to control their minds,
yet, without that control, what we learn will not be
retained. You will develop and discipline your mind
power in a very short time, which you would have
expected only from years of practice, and economize

on energy in the process. It is surprising how much our efficiency can be improved by the cultivation of an orderly mind, which, if less hurried, can concentrate on matters adequately at all times. When we learn to turn from hustle and hurry to the habit of a mental quietness, we gain its first reward, the soothing of our nerves. And the more effort you put into it, the more likely you are to have positive results. You will develop the capacity to bring your activities into a stable obedience, and through that to bring your mind to a conscious steadiness, necessary to overcome negative distractions. The results will be proportionate to the amount of effort you put into it.

We are separated from each other only by our own individual habits, but our natures are generally the same. If, instead of striving to change our nature, we move more slowly and steadily, our entire outlook will improve, and a complete confidence in our ability to change our habits will result. You will find the mere change of pace will produce maximum productivity out of each moment. Probably new technological innovations, such as fax machines, which save us time, have increased our demands for faster tempos and hectic schedules. We wonder why they do not seem to ease our time pressures, as these new technologies were invented to save work and provide more leisure. If we slow down, we can liberate ourselves from our old behaviour by revealing our true desires to ourselves. In the same way, when our mind relaxes, our attentiveness to our thoughts are increased. We can be our own handicap, and those who are continually rushing exhaust themselves quickly, as they put too much strain on their energy and allow themselves no time to determine which of their activities deserve priority. By controlling our own speed, we will be sensitive to what tempo is suitable to bring about conditions for the fulfilment of our potential. The satisfaction of using our faculties to the full is a basic requirement for achieving self-assurance. It reinforces our confidence that results must come, as everything which is permanent in life is a result of slow growth. Hurry will prevent the development of this growth as it will increase the possibility of our pursuing misguided aims.

With your new tempo, a more controlled self will be of more benefit to your life and diminish the consequences of life-long negative habits. To cure yourself of these habits permanently, a successful method is to rid yourself of old behaviours and simultaneously replace them with new ones. This is easy if you devote your efforts to a new disciplined pace. **You cannot control all the circumstances in your life, but you can control your attitude towards them**, with a proven enlightened technique. It is an excellent mode of mind training, which strengthens your capacity for continued concentration and will greatly diminish your concern about the outcome of problems. It is a goal which you are capable of achieving, and is a principle to which most successful people attribute their success in life and in their careers. Without it, you will never succeed.

In order to lead a productive life it is necessary to have proper mental control. You can achieve it simply through the practice of a reduced tempo. When your mind is calm and your body relaxed, important things cease to be a chore, as you will have time to anticipate them and be more inclined to deal with them suitably as they appear. It is like a new indestructable peace, you will now do everything effortlessly as you begin to realize that permanent success is possible if it is built on a carefully arranged foundation. There are many obstacles in life and practising this very excellent mode of mind training will help you overcome the stressful ones by controlling your response to them. People with a faster tempo consistently form the habit of looking too far ahead and neglect to enjoy the present. Only our present moment exists, in fact, and unless we proceed at a normal steady pace, the original aspirations for any of our high ideals will be forgotten. **You cannot rush through your life expecting happiness only in the future.** If you believe time is precious and that you waste it thoughtlessly by doing things slowly, you are wrong. You will achieve your aims much faster and certainly be less vulnerable to failure, if you slow down. You will be improving your time-management, which involves arranging tasks in order of importance. In this new world of hustle, we have a phobia about wasting time. However, some of the most productive hours one spends can appear useless to others, who may view contemplative people as time wasters. Artists, writers and other creative people spend periods of time idling, preparing to receive ideas from the subconscious mind. The time which some may describe as wasted, could prove to be the most productive and could be described as a productive procrastination. The secret is to live every moment relaxed. Often, the time waiting for planes or delayed trips can be usefully utilized in viewing our life's perspective. People who know how to control the pace of their activities may receive some important hunches while waiting in a traffic jam, in direct contrast to those whose impatience at the traffic and frustration about the delay increases their stress level. When you are relaxed, you establish a new mind equilibrium. Your thoughts will become more keenly concentrated, which will be noticeable in your everyday actions.

You will acquire a poise and calm which will be immediately apparent through these efforts, enabling you to deal with everything in a positive way. **Learn how to possess each day by first taking possession of yourself.**

GO SLOWLY WITH YOUR AIMS IN
VIEW, THE WORLD BELONGS TO
THE PATIENT MAN.

PLATO

What You Can Conceive, You Can Achieve
Through Intuition

5

Trusting your inner voice and trusting life are the
same thing, we have to learn to be attentive to our
intuition, the part of us that contains our innate
wisdom. We are not isolated individuals, there is an
invisible force within us which can channel creative
intuitional messages and which transcends our
normal conscious thinking, if we train our minds to
be receptive.

We can all gain access to productive powers,
which can lead us to a way of life beyond our
imagination, and which can be achieved with much
less energy than we are at presently using. If you
learn to control your thoughts, these powers can be
acquired very easily just by concentrating your
attention on a specific problem. How you solve your
everyday situations is what counts; if you train your

mind to think intuitively, you will solve them sooner and the answers will appear much clearer.

Creative people understand they can succeed in any field even where others have failed, and we can succeed too, if we fulfil the necessary conditions. If we understand how our mind can function creatively to inspire intuition, we can avoid situations which require logical decisions that are usually arrived at through a long process.

We are all aware of possessing some degree of creativity, significant or otherwise, but do we know that we can assist this process by learning more about our subconscious mind? Our creative levels generally do their work subconsciously. We should consciously search inside ourselves for what is authentic and accept that as a guide to cultivating our awareness and sensitivity to responding appropriately to every situation we encounter, and learn the art of listening to our inner self. **The more we trust that inner self, the more it grows.**

We can gain experience and translate ideas into reality just by training our conscious and subconscious minds to cooperate with each other, as you would expect two partners to behave. It is exactly like a partnership. Your conscious mind is sending down its unsolved problems to its partner, the subconscious mind, which will use its files of past experiences to search for a solution. Creative people understand this technique and, as a result, have developed confidence in themselves which enables them to improve their circumstances. We should constantly be alert to hunches, which will appear when we least expect them. You will find that fresh ideas will continue to flow out of nowhere and your new creativeness will seem to be following orders, stimulated to heights beyond expectations.

To conquer yourself is not to obtain power over other people, but to have an ability to live a full life, which entails an understanding of its vulnerability and needs. You should be alert to your subconscious mind. Examine the ideas that come to you. Once you have gathered information about an idea, mull it over and let the information incubate for a time until your subsconscious produces flashes of insight. With controlled attention, you put your accurate thinking into action by evaluating the good and the bad consequences. If you master this simple principle, you will form new positive habits. **All successful people radiate positive attitudes, which may even inspire others to assist them to realize their dreams.**

We have to learn to have faith in our intuition, the part of our subconscious mind that knows and retains all our past experiences and is ready at all times to provide information requested by our conscious mind. Deep down inside, we are all psychic, and definitely not alone. Our minds are full of energies floating around, and whether we choose to use them and to what degree is entirely up to our expectations.

A sure ingredient for the successful use of your intuitive powers is to have a purpose or a goal in your life. There is no better road for happiness than to have a planned direction with a discipline to support it. This will encourage you to develop your inner resources, thereby increasing your powers of intuition. A motivated purpose in life is the greatest incentive for inspiration as it instils an enthusiasm. Success is a habit and you can form the habit of success by practising positive principles. If you tend towards negative thinking, you are not likely to succeed in cultivating your intuition.

Intuition is receiving solutions to problems which, up to now, seemed unsolvable; they are hunches which come to you from nowhere. You may believe you are unable to trace the source, as it is a mysterious force, but intuition is within us all and is a result of practising in a concentrated way. Once you have cultivated your intuition, receiving its messages will not come as a surprise; on the contrary, you will be expecting them, as you will have developed a new found mental confidence and your outlook on life will become brighter. They are authentic responses, arising from an awareness of what is going on around you.

Intuition is a product of a developed mind which has been trained to become proficient in concentrating on a specific problem, or on the solution to a particular situation by developing a capacity for continued attention. If you withdraw yourself from unproductive issues, which are not immediate and can be attended to at some other time, and concentrate your attention on your main objective, you will develop this force within you. If you identify and concentrate on this objective, an intuitive feeling will be induced by your mind being held steady in a receptive state enabling it to receive messages that will aid you in a solution. These messages will be channelled into your mind without your striving too hard.

This process will become more effective if you

regulate your speed, which will give you more time for a reflective method of working. You cannot force your mind to come up with quick answers, and if you do you will fail as your behaviour will prevent your receiving inspiring revelations from your sub-conscious. Your thoughts must not be hurried, if your mind is to be alert to positive ideas. Your intuition has to be nourished slowly. We all possess artistic and creative potential and, if we learn to tune into this, we will be amazed at the possibly limitless potential lying dormant within us. If we learn to use our creative powers, revelations will continually appear, which, if we follow them, will lead us to our goals. You will not obtain the best results through intuition unless you exercise disciplined control over your mind, as you are less likely to awaken inner powers if your energies are scattered.

When you know at what pace you function the best, as with any new conduct, adherence to the practice alone is a sure means of success and a means to inspiration, which can then be used as a stimulus to create achievement in any field. The technique is to hold on to the picture of your desired goals, and intuition will then provide ways of achieving them. **The secret of success, is to remember that success**

depends on keeping your aims in view and not letting them fade away. Your mind will become more concentrated as a new inner serenity will be brought into your working life, and you will now be capable of approaching your work with a new focused attention, as you will think actively about an idea until it is fully explored. You may even begin to feel the presence of a higher power and reassess meanings of important past experiences, understanding them now more fully. Your thoughts will cease to wander off, as you adopt a new reflective attitude towards your future, and the greatest pleasure will be experienced when you realize you have mastered this technique. You will find you have become more tranquil and your temperament more placid, your concentration and awareness will be improved, and you will be able to work for longer periods without fatigue.

Cultivating your intuition will ultimately increase your vitality and enable you to maintain good health. Intuition can alert you to early warnings or danger signals concerning your health, and protect you from squandering your energies as you will be more sensitive to your body and receptive to your feelings. It will regulate your expenditure of energies and guard against your wasting more time than is necessary on a project. You will find that stress will now disappear and a new intense exhilaration will replace it. Of course, in some instances it could also help you recognize the necessity of increasing your energy for other projects. We can be more successful in meeting challenges if we ration physical and mental energies.

As we analyse our problems more deeply, the incubation period of ideas between your conscious and subconscious mind will be shorter, as they will be more mutually co-operative and you will work out your solutions effortlessly. You will realize that making full use of your subconscious storehouse of knowledge and past experiences will prove to be most effective in alerting your mind to creative inspiration. Your mind will now be organizing your intuition so that it continues to grow richer in content. It is a simple way of working with your inner mind. The practice of regulating your tempo will leave your mind open to receive these flashes of illumination. When you consciously see your desires in a mind picture, your subconscious mind will send important messages to assist you in completing them. If you reflect on the matter, you will have a fuller perception of its meaning and deal with each situation as it arises, using intuition to throw light on each problem. You have to trust your intuition's sudden flashes of understanding, which can appear at any time.

Your striving to achieve an intuitive state must be accompanied by self-discipline. New activities stimulate the mind and exercise the brain. Living by habit alone, and doing the same thing each day reduces your ability to become creative. Even a modest decision like making a change in your reading material, instead of habitually reading of light material, can be a way of brain building. Books which help in the development of your intuition can also be a new and satisfying interest. And conversely, a person may become ineffective after moving from a job which requires much thought to one that requires very little.

We derive a lot of self-esteem by doing a job well and being rewarded for it. An unhappy work situation discourages our self-esteem and can cause our interest to fade away as we lose our incentives. If you fail to keep up-to-date in your field you will know less and less each year and your knowledge will eventually become a thing of the past. If you fail to maintain your wisdom and judgement, you will find that abilities can become obsolete if they are not kept alive. One of the main reasons for a lack of wide-ranging interests is an inability to strive for anything that is not of practical importance to one's finances. Those who love their work retain their experience more successfully than those who do not.

Cultivating new interests gives us a sense of proportion, as we find relief in other matters. The temporary change of thought provides an opportunity for the subconscious to digest problems more accurately, as our subconscious works more effectively when we are asleep or occupied with other matters. The time you take to turn your mind from a perplexing matter to something else can be a moment when you develop your intuitional powers. What occurs in the mechanics of your brain cannot easily be explained. But your accumulation of experiences is limitless and can solve many situations. With discipline, you learn to analyse each problem concentrating and thinking things through to their solution.

Forgetting your work when it is over and becoming involved in other interests will improve your creativity more than constantly worrying about the same thing and ending your day exhausted. We have all experienced problems which have appeared to have no solution in sight. At such times, the ability to direct your attention to other matters and become absorbed in interests which are not connected to the problem is of substantial benefit. Your intuition functions at all times and is even more inspiring when you are not consciously forcing the answers. The more relaxed you are, the more favourable are the conditions for co-operation between your conscious and subconscious mind.

We are not likely to solve our problems successfully if we are fatigued or worried. It is better, therefore, sometimes to forget the problem worrying for a while and concentrate on different activities. By doing this, we are more open to signals coming from within, and we can listen to and respect our own insights and intuitions. When the problem is re-examined later, we may have a new perspective. The mind often resolves issues when we are not thinking about them. Creative people call it incubating an idea. If we are constantly preoccupied with insignificant matters, we will never experience the quiet time necessary to develop these powers. **When we give undivided attention to our inner voice, we find we**

have an ally whose support and comfort will remain with us for the rest of our life.

BETTER KEEP YOURSELF CLEAN
AND BRIGHT. YOU ARE THE
WINDOW THROUGH WHICH YOU
MUST SEE THE WORLD.

GEORGE BERNARD SHAW

Faith Without Religion

6

As religion is accepted as a primary source of emotional security, it could be an affront to popular opinion and may even be considered offensive that many people are sincerely searching for a substitute for the generally accepted religious faiths, as they hold the view that the existence of any external order beyond this world is without logical support or meaning. These searchers are also disenchanted with the lifestyle of many religious leaders who, as a result of media scrutiny, have destroyed confidence in their responsibility to be the chief guardians of our souls. This has resulted in an inability for some people to attain solace in traditional faiths.

The disparity between some religious leaders' preaching and their personal behaviour is very wide. In fact, it is utterly at variance with logic of common sense. Obviously, in many cases, their main concern is their own self-interest. The information disclosed in recent scandals give point to that judgement.

As sceptics struggle with religious doubts, questioning the validity of religion and asserting themselves against its complexities and confusions, many are ready to search for a better philosophy to replace the old faiths that do not satisfy their intellectual needs and which they believe are immature. They question not only these so-called religious leaders who have succeeded in acquiring power over them by claiming they are God's representatives on earth, but also their ambiguous explanations of religious teachings and rituals. As well as instilling a guilt or fear of divine retribution if we do not subordinate ourselves to a disciplined compliance, they expect an obedience and reverence because they alone have contact with some higher power which has control over our destiny. Their teachings are, however, in many cases completely contradictory to their personal, moral and ethical conduct and appeal mainly to those who have an overwhelming need to believe in some unexplainable force.

Freud dismissed religion as a neurotic illusion. However, there are spiritual philosophies in the East, which although they do not teach the existence of God, are extremely beneficial to our mental health as they teach us how to work out our own salvation. They deliberately reject any belief which does not deal with reality and have a more popular appeal among those who are attracted to a culturally productive way of life.

These philosophies require study, self-discipline and mind development, which aid the cultivation of intuition. They guide you to a more practical approach to a philosophical and spiritual goal. They cannot be followed by the mere acceptance of blind faith or that which could be viewed as an illusion. There are no blood stains in their histories, which are almost three thousand years old, and in no instances have they ever attempted to destroy other faiths by criticism or force, or even the display of religious symbols, which is a common characteristic of the well-known religions.

The sources of purity and goodness are within us. We all know the difference between good and evil, and we are able if we wish to translate this knowledge into our everyday activities. We need to recognize that we can find our own personal interpretation of God within ourselves, and this will unlock the spirituality dormant in us.

Why the continual search for God? Has the God we generally perceive made a valuable contribution to mankind, or has He actually produced substantial harm? How much carnage has been committed in His name? This is a very reasonable question, in view of the fact that, in the past and even up to the present day, many millions of innocent people have experienced unspeakable horrors, some of which have ended in extermination, because of their religion, the adherence to which was merely an accident of birth.

Some religious leaders, who claim infallability and that supreme truth is determined and defined by them, are consciously engaged in the promotion of ill-will, and have encouraged intolerance of particular religions instead of teaching ways of minimizing or discouraging hatreds. On any given day, it is possible to find instances of killings or extensive bomb damage causing the death of innocent people in the name of religion somewhere in the world. Often these killings are committed against people of other religions. The religions they adhere to decide on how those of other faiths are to be perceived, either as people to be loved or to be destroyed.

Practically all religions claim they are the only true one and dare to pass judgement on others. Have they examined every religion, which I very much doubt, and if so, how do they know they have chosen the best?

Many scholars, educated philosophers and intellectuals believe that we have an inner peace, and that we ourselves can relieve our anxieties and solve our complexes by learning a proven technique that can not only teach us to work out our own salvation, but will produce a new spiritual power which will help purge ourselves of self-illusion. We need to find a purpose to our existence. Within us we can find a vision or a voice to tell us how to fulfil our desires and guide us in our present life.

Many people believe that worshipping is no longer sufficient and feel particularly ill-at-ease with the idea of directly praying to some outside source. The decline in church attendance testifies to that. Religions that claim to represent the same God are so hopelessly divided among themselves they have only one thing in common: their differences. They are unable to provide logical explanations for their existence and only mystical answers are offered to those questions.

Faith Without Religion

Are there parallels between some religions as organizations of power and totalitarian countries bent on dominating peoples' minds? They are, although very different, both patterns of power which deny freedom of thought in their organizations. Both claim they are guardians of our culture. They manufacture elaborate publicity machines for their followers, which produce the same results. Their primary objective is a contrived adulation. They, and they alone, determine what is right or wrong. On the one hand is a cultivated obedience to believe; on the other, a demand to obey. Either you will be punished by the state, or will fear divine retribution.

We know that the human mind can be conditioned to accept things as truth. Some religious leaders, who insist it is a sin for God to be idolized, nevertheless amass untold wealth with impunity, which then is brought to our attention by disclosures of sexual and financial scandals. Hundreds of millions of dollars are collected by them, often by vigorous demands, tax free, with which they maintain their highly extravagant standard of living, without being compelled to account to anybody for the money they receive or how it was spent.

Very often tricks are employed to collect religious

contributions. In America some television evangelists regularly claim miraculous healings through a personal prayer to God on your behalf, but only after you call in with your donation. A cheque has to be promised for each prayer performed; charge and credit cards accepted. Cripples are shown being pushed to the stage in wheelchairs. We are informed they have been invalids for years. They then walk off the stage on their own legs, cured, and their wheelchairs are ceremoniously destroyed. The exact same procedure is used with men leaning heavily on walking sticks and proceeding slowly to the stage. The Evangelist touches a forehead, uttering a prayer with his eyes closed. Within minutes the stick is no longer needed and is broken into two pieces. You would assume that people would question if they could be mailing their money to the wrong address; after all, if God performed these miracles, are these ministers not presumptuous in deciding that they are to be the proponents of them? And there may be others who are equally desperate for miracles, but cannot afford the donation. Why should they be excluded?

Jim Bakker was sentenced to a prison term for defrauding his followers of 158 million dollars over and above his regular religious collections in one specific scheme.

The Reverend Oral Roberts claimed in 1987 that God would end his life if his followers did not contribute four and a half million dollars in one appeal. He was obviously successful, as he is still alive.

General William Booth, of the Salvation Army, and his daughter were sued for millions of pounds by his son, who claims he was entitled to one third of their wealth, as he was associated with them in previous charity organizations, which were unsuccessful, and claimed that he should have been rightfully included in the Salvation Army. When he supplied evidence to the court of vast monies held by them in banks in various countries, they settled out of court for an undisclosed amount, and the son was then elected a general of the Salvation Army, with an income and expenses worthy of that position.

Television Evangelist, Jimmy Swaggert, openly sobbed in a television presentation, confessing tearfully that he had sinned, after it was disclosed he had been seen with a prostitute in a motel. His religious rival, who had followed him there and exposed him, had been previously accused of exactly the same thing by Jimmy Swaggert himself. Obviously he was eager to censure human errors and follies in others, while concealing his own.

You can very simply enfold your own spiritual self, your mind holds undreamed of inner powers that can be used to create the life you want. This is inherent in all of us, without surrendering ourselves to organized beliefs which are beyond our control. You can directly experience an understanding of your own soul by exploring deeper and more satisfying levels of your true self with its sudden intuitive flashes of understanding. If you take time to think, and in particular to face yourself, you will be challenging your old faiths and accepting alternative objects of admiration — your own ability to utilize the power available to you each day. This is not easy for most of us, we can be uncomfortable looking deeply into ourselves; although we will make constructive decisions if we are honest with our self-appraisal.

It can be compared to looking into a mirror you have just cleaned, and seeing yourself clearly for the first time. If you persevere with this process, you will approach life's problems effectively. You can deal with most of your worries by creating a coherent system of thought to relate to a better philosophy of living. **Tranquillity of mind can be achieved when you learn to conquer yourself by directing your own destiny or your own soul,** simply by learning a mental discipline which will keep you in control of your thoughts.

Know your own true nature and acknowledge your self-defeating faults. You must create your own environment and master your situations, whatever they are. You can produce your own sense of security when you acquire confidence in your ability to create your future as you wish it; the power is already in you. You have the right to make your own choices, all you have to do is to learn how you can function for your own benefit by having a belief in yourself. **All we are, is the result of what we have thought.** If the thoughts are right, the right actions will follow and things will then go smoothly and somewhat pleasantly, leading us to a richer and fuller life, through learning to take responsibility for our own condition. The chapters in this book on positive thinking and the power of intuition can be of great assistance to you in finding a new faith in yourself and achieving a better way of life.

Prayers are not always the solution for the world's

dilemmas; the world is not stable, it contains many pleasant and some undesirable situations. We cannot spend our whole life resisting that which is inevitable. Under these circumstances, the life we live may at times be conflicting but we should not expect to be happy every day of our lives. To hope to have no problems is to work against life. As Lord Byron said, "There is not a joy the world can give like that it takes away."

Most of the problems in this world are eventually controlled or cured by human effort, not by clinging to monotonous creeds and dogmas, which are far from reality. Of course, we have not been able to prevent devastating wars, and have been unsuccessful in curbing an ever-increasing crime rate; obviously, prayers have been equally unsuccessful. Life's problems can seem overwhelming at times, but difficulties can be overcome or diminished by marshalling the powerful forces of your mind in a positive way, and refusing to give in to defeating thoughts by replacing them with a constructive outlook.

Enlightened minds have understood it is possible to tap the subconscious mind to draw on past experiences for the right decisions, which is an essential ingredient in conquering yourself. Facing up to our true self will open a door to these experiences; after all, our representation of God is unconsciously organized by our own minds. Is the subconscious giving the same message as religion without its supernatural content? The ability to solve problems, creative or practical, is influenced by the knowledge available in our subconscious mind. It is the custodian of our past, of every thought, every past decision that was successful and the ones which were not. If used intuitively it can be the most powerful tool at your command. Intuition is not a mysterious force, but a skilled resource in utilizing your inner wisdom. It just requires learning to connect your conscious and subconscious awareness systems, which affect much of what you do or think.

It is possible to have faith in your subconscious mind, as you would have a belief in any religion, without the rituals which accompany it; especially when it can produce all the answers for your salvation. Praying has the similar effect of releasing your power of optimism. If I had to design a new religion, I would advocate this technique for its fulfilment. This religion would also be based on the principle of a philosophy in which all abilities could be utilized to the full, merely by creating a new method of behaviour.

It would be acknowledged as part of reality, and not as some power standing apart from us. Its essential feature would be a constructive and positive attitude of mind, used in conjunction with the vast files of experiences stored in our subconscious. With or without religion, **life will always be empty if we fail to have a purpose** and, therefore, we should first plan our own special destiny.

If we fear misfortune, we must learn to deal with it ourselves and not wait for an outside source to come to our rescue. There is no greater obstacle to sound judgement than fear. If you expect the worst, you are opening the door to it. If you intend to take control of your life in whatever way you can, you will be preparing for the best. Those who have a strong sense that they can control their own lives are more likely to prevent misfortune, as they have confidence in their ability to survive.

First we must imagine our worst fear. When we realize that maybe its coming will not be such a disaster the fear will be reduced significantly. **The more you analyse the cause of the fear, the less it will control you.** The technique then, is to seek for the answer by diagnosing the problem correctly, yet to remain physically relaxed. The effort of identifying solely with the object of your thoughts will produce results.

When you have thought through the problem consciously and failed to arrive at a solution, your mind will then feed it to your subconscious, which will return answers based on the information you feed it. The final solution generally comes to you intuitively. Creative thinkers know these procedures are the benefit of an intuitive awareness, and if they are successful in their profession, it is as a result of using these powers. This is something we can all develop, if we relax and do not force our minds for immediate answers. With its continual practice, your mind will be developed to its full potential and will come up with solutions to perplexing problems effortlessly in due time.

When using this technique, it is wise not to spend the intervening or incubating time thinking about the problem. Devote your mind to other matters, dismissing that particular problem from your mind as you have done all you can for the present, and besides, your mental processes very often work when you are asleep. How often have you heard the expression, "I will sleep on it"?

It has been claimed that these results are in reality directed by God and the inner guidance or voice speaking to us from within comes from that source. This is incorrect. If psychic phenomena exist, there is no reason to claim they cannot be studied scientifically to find reasonable explanations. Science is concerned with many things which are not claiming to be supernatural. It is entirely systematic common sense, and is a method of attuning yourself to an inner life or opening a door to a new awareness. A result of developing one's own mind proficiently is to achieve answers on any subject, which are normally inaccessible to the average mind. **You will now have a new power which you yourself can control.** If you feel you have been hampered by being deprived of the consolation of religious beliefs, you will now be compensated.

This technique, however, is not to be used only at times of crisis or to overcome serious obstacles, it should be maintained at all times as a new way of life to master everyday situations. As Aristotle said, "You are what you habitually do." As I have said, it is similar to having a silent partner, who controls the vast storehouse of information in your subconscious mind and whose sole concern is the responsibility of working out your problems.

Is it beyond comprehension that those with difficulties who frequently pray are merely triumphing over adversity by unknowingly appealing to the subconscious mind? **Is it the subconscious mind with intuitive answers that people believe to be God?**

MINDS ARE NOT CONQUERED BY
ARMS OR DOGMAS, BUT BY GREAT-
NESS OF SOUL.

SPINOZA

Growing Old is a Bad Habit

7

As we live, we continuously age physically. It is a process we are incapable of preventing, and we accept this as an indispensable condition with the passing of years, if we wish to survive. It is certainly better than the alternative, but few of us welcome it with enthusiasm. However, people are ageing better than ever before and are generally healthier, which has extended our life expectancy.

Oscar Wilde, in his poignant story of "The picture of Dorian Grey", transfers this process to a portrait of Dorian Grey, who attempts to maintain his youth permanently while his portrait ages. In real life, it is our portraits which remain the same and we who age.

This process of ageing does not necessarily have to apply to our minds; studies have shown that acquiring vital absorbing interests will not only extend our youth, but by utilizing our abilities to the full we will be rewarded by prolonging it. The more we gradually expand our knowledge and acquire more interests, the more our intelligence is increased. Added knowledge and experience will maintain a youthful conception of life. **People don't stop learning because they grow old, they grow old because they stop learning.**

If we search out new interests and prepare new objectives for the future, the longer our youthful energy will be sustained. If you live a monotonous life, your mind will acquire a dullness, proportionate to the extent of your inactivity. But an interest will create an optimistic awareness, and you will age less quickly if you have a valid reason for living. Mental activity contributes to your physical and mental well being, which may be a factor in why some people age more than others and seem to remain much healthier.

We do not have to settle for unproductive lives in our later years, we can enjoy diverse interests by deliberately making the effort to stimulate our minds into a higher level of vitality. We generate our own energy and retirement can be used as an opportunity not for idleness, but for creativity. If we undertake work that is stimulating, we improve our brain activity, which in turn will lead to a highly creative state and produce a more interesting life, avoiding an everyday state of dull passiveness. Regardless of age, there could be a wonderful new world waiting for us.

There is nothing more dull than a retired person without work and without interests. Every one has a talent, which if undeveloped, they secretly desire to utilize. Having more leisure time creates a perfect opportunity to pursue these desires either as a hobby, or as an income producing pastime, or both. There is no reason why an elderly person should not launch out on a new career, just because the establishment disapproves. New interests are also necessary to prevent boredom and having interesting work is far superior to the emptiness you feel when you have nothing to do. Besides, when work is interesting, it is capable of giving greater satisfaction than merely providing relief from boredom.

Retired people often accept menial jobs far below their knowledge and experience. This is a mistake, as they are aware of how precious time is and should be more discriminating of its use. The elderly have numerous skills which include a preparedness for crisis and practical experience. There should be no legal barriers for people over a certain age, who wish to remain in the work force.

It is reasonable to want to retire, that is quite natural. But if retired people decide to return to the work force, they should continue to improve their skills and knowledge and not accept menial work. Their continued employment and education are of benefit not only to themselves but also to others, as they contribute what skills they possess to the common good.

There are two possible obstacles. The first is that our age may be a deterrent in applying for an executive position. And the second may be that we will not want to invest our capital on a new venture in later years. Both of them can easily be overcome. There are many retired people who have decided to return to employment by operating from their home, and have not only become more successful, but have accomplished everything with half the energy, time and expense they previously expended. This has allowed them more time for leisure. They have contacts from their previous business life and save considerably on expense of office space and other expenses. Add to that, the availability of techno-logically advanced business equipment at an insignificant outlay, such as fax machines, answering machines, computers and sophisticated telephone equipment; and last but not least, people who have retired from business already have sufficient income for their needs and do not have to continually worry about finances. And although they are using their home as a base, access to all that equipment means the whole world is spread out before them and they can still fully employ their skills.

The person who pursues a wisely directed maturity will aim for a number of interests, other than those required for the maintenance of living necessities. It is of course of primary importance to have a sufficient income to provide for all the essentials for the family. Outside interests will provide opportunities to alleviate any misfortunes which may arise. At such times, the capacity to redirect our interests to other matters will reduce the pressures or anxieties and help us relax back into ourselves, especially when there is nothing that can be done about the problem for the time being.

As we age, our perception of what we really want in life becomes clearer and it is easier to focus our attention and energy into obtaining it. We no longer expect to be perfect and are not unduly disappointed by the fact that we are not. Therefore, coping with difficult situations will be less stressful. Many people have been deceived by a so-called youth oriented culture into believing that young people have more opportunity for mental advancement. On the contrary, it is never too late to apply effort towards improvement at any age. **The beginning of life's experiences cannot compare with a lifetime of past experiences.**

The brain is equally manageable at any age; a stimulating environment will improve your thinking ability. There is no difference between the potential of people in their twenties or those in their seventies, as elderly people have more power than they believe possible. They should be reminded that they probably have resources which have been lying dormant in them, and should plan to bring them to the surface. Their creativeness can be full of surprises, and there should be no concern about challenging themselves by setting higher goals than they believe possible. Many successful people have discovered that the way to get ahead is deliberately to seek out more than you expect.

Any action is obviously superior to no action. Action produces an awareness, which becomes deeper as you exert more effort. And action is capable of giving the pleasure of achievement, as you will now be more usefully employed. It is important to realize that a strong belief in yourself releases more energy and unveils an inherent ability to conquer yourself, by moving in a planned direction. We can all have the same determination, regardless of age.

We are never aware of what is our best, until we attempt to find out by pushing to the limit of our capabilities. Wisdom, judgement and the advantages of leisure time are all necessary in finding a new zest for living and enhancing our brainpower, if we wish to become personally enriched. Retirement produces opportunities for a change in pace and occupation. With children gone, loneliness and boredom can appear without warning. Regardless of age, having a purpose in life is essential for a continued personal growth. Besides keeping us active, it can be a useful distraction from minor frustrations and helps us maintain our self-esteem.

Learning new things is a sure way to stay young; older people have the advantage of access to years of personal and professional information which can aid the kind of deep thinking required for problem solving. They are also more at peace with themselves and usually are not burdened with the anxieties of younger people. We would all like to continue to maintain our faculties as we age. Although we are undoubtedly living longer, we should not assume this means spending more time in old age; on the contrary, it should mean we have a longer youthful age.

Contrary to popular belief, today's senior citizens are much younger than their chronological age, as the prospects for continuing good health, energy and longer life are much better than they were in our parents' days. We therefore have more time to pursue new interests or improve existing ones, and cannot claim lack of time as an excuse.

In fact, claiming to have not enough time is an avoidance tactic. The first step is always the hardest and once started a project will develop its own momentum. Besides, our past knowledge will be wasted if we do not open our minds to new challenges, as our brains tend to get rusty, if they are not stimulated.

We have to understand which activities bring us the most pleasure and what we enjoy learning more about. It is important to recognize which areas do not need strengthening, and which areas we believe we should develop and the skills we require to cultivate in order to master them. We are then able to embark on a new lifestyle that will allow fulfilment of our interests and desires.

We have to change our negative perceptions of the ageing process and acknowledge that the general conceptions of our old age are not true. Characteristics that are assumed to be an inevitable result of ageing, may merely be the result of the disuse and inactivity of our minds. Now is the time to satisfy our secret inner longings, when we should give these longings a positive force instead of fantasizing about them. We are limited only by the state of our mind, and the beliefs formed throughout our life, not by the pessimistic age-old myths about growing old.

The most important ingredient for staying young is simply to employ your time wisely and allow your knowledge and experience to grow with living. Elderly people are becoming more active than in previous generations and, more importantly, are more secure and independent as they are free of the responsibilities of raising a family. **Growing old should be treated as a bad habit, which a busy person has no time to form.**

If we utilize our subconscious storehouse of past

experiences, our later years can be the most satisfying period of our lives. Regardless of our age, and if we recognize the valuable assets we have and use them for the furthering of our career, more opportunities can appear. Increased knowledge is a door to personal enrichment and self-sufficiency and can reveal new horizons, previously believed unobtainable. By continuing to seek to improve, you will become part of the future, not just a part of the past.

We need not fear making mistakes. With careful thinking, most of them can be avoided, although it is important to realize even mistakes have their use. They teach us what works and what does not. **Most successful people have profited from their mistakes, and from turning failure into success.** Changing your priorities also does not mean you have not succeeded; your needs may change, therefore your priorities should change with them. Those who have failed to realize their potential are not necessarily lacking in it, they just have not discovered how to achieve it. The chapter on intuition will explain a technique to bring potential to the surface on an intuitional level. It will teach you how to release untapped sources of energy, increase your creativity and encourage you to discover your true inner feelings, by learning to know yourself.

It is evident, as one advances in years, that the improvement of our abilities and the furthering of our interests can be extremely therapeutic. The more interests we have, the more opportunities exist for enjoying life, as we are less concerned with how to fill our days. If one area of interest becomes less satisfactory, then there are many others to replace it; and besides, **when you have many interests, you become an object of interest to others.**

There are many late achievers who have found that continuous leisure is more intolerable than continuous work, and who discovered that the cure for old age is simply, not to abandon life too soon. In many cases, their creative achievements have reached far beyond the average person, and they have maintained their health, vitality and longevity by the work they have produced. They provide the evidence of what can be achieved when we use our abilities to the full and do not surrender ourselves to idleness. Old age can be the most satisfying period in your life.

Growing Old is a Bad Habit

IDLENESS IS A HOLIDAY FOR
FOOLS.

CHINESE PROVERB

Success Without Stress

8

There is very little sense in achieving success in one field only, if all the other activities or spheres in your life are a dismal failure. A person's success is generally measured by their money and possessions. The respect a person commands is in proportion to their wealth; the greater the wealth, the greater the respect. Logically, people should only be admired for their good character; their possessions are just part of their environment.

Genuine success is achieving a balanced life style, one in which we have fulfilled ourselves in all aspects, while retaining the capacity to maintain an equilibrium undisturbed by any fear of stress. This in turn will benefit not only ourselves but those around us. Acquiring a tranquil mind is just as important as acquiring material wealth, especially when we have more than sufficient for our needs and could, if we chose, have permanent leisure with security. **What good are possessions if they are too dearly earned** and we have to continually struggle in order to add to them? They serve no purpose other than magnifying our own ego and, in many cases, the price paid for them does not compensate for the benefits received.

If we free ourselves from the pursuit of more money than we can possibly spend, we will find life more gratifying. We will be wasting less energy and will secure a self-confidence which will better equip us to overcome adversity than will the mere accumulation of money to the exclusion of everything else. Of course, money can be a necessary ingredient for happiness, but it is a mistake to ignore the other ingredients, which may be of equal importance. Achieving success may prove to be a startling paradox. Difficulties that seem to bar the path to achievement may in the end prove to be the beginning of a more profound success. Learning how to set realistic goals can be one of the most important factors in overcoming difficulties.

The absence of a prepared plan for your future can result in a feeling of emptiness. If you stop moving, life will also stop. There are many forms of stress in our lives, which can wear us down. If you learn to cultivate a deliberately calm approach to life, the inner serenity achieved will be carried on into your work and personal life, and you will prevent many stressful situations arising. This calmness will reward you by releasing skills which, prior to now, you were unaware you possessed, and promoting an efficiency and wisdom which make it easier to function effectively in the real world.

Stress can be described as a physical response to demands which you perceive as threatening; the tensions are more than your body can handle. Even boredom can produce stress, as you will be continually comparing it with more pleasurable times. When people are trapped in an empty life they forego the opportunity to be occupied with challenging programmes, and succumb to their natural tendency to become discouraged if there is nothing positive in sight. The knowledge that we are not improving or developing can keep our spirits low. The cure is to keep in touch with our real needs, reorganizing our life, questioning if all our routine habits are really necessary and finding new stimulating interests to replace them.

Boredom can be an opportunity in disguise, as it

can produce incentives to take up new interests. Life will be more meaningful if you have an objective and a planned method to achieve it. **It is not the events which occur in our lives that cause stress, it is the manner in which we respond to them, which produces symptoms of stress.** The circumstances which appear fearful to some are merely irksome to others, who have more perseverance and more patience.

There is a proven method of coping with stress under all conditions. When pressures start building up you should immediately relax every part of your body and this will automatically greatly reduce the intensity of the stress, or even eliminate it. This is an old Yogi formula which can improve your health and contribute to the quality of your life. Stress is always more severe when you are full of tension.

Many of us become over-stressed by our reaction to negative remarks by other people. Often their hostile attitude encourages us to respond with anger, thus causing ourselves stress. Our refusal to answer by completely ignoring them will prevent stress, as they will have failed in their attempt to aggravate us. Constraint is a more effective response than automatic counter-attack. This can only succeed in irritating us, and frustrates us physically and emotionally, as our reactions affect our body behaviour and our thoughts. If we lose our sense of control, our chances of responding intelligently are remote and will adversely affect our response.

No one will agree with you all the time, nor will you understand others at all times. If you expect those around you to approve of everything you say, you are heading for a life of frustration and fear of criticism from others can cause tension. Their hostility may hurt, but you can avoid it causing you stress by refusing to allow it to disrupt your life. A "could not care less attitude" will be very effective in releasing you from tensions, and not only will others respect you but, more importantly, you will respect yourself. Badly expressed anger can be a further source of stress. If you find that being in particular company is provoking and an underlying cause of unhappiness, it would be advisable to take a good look at your own behaviour or attitude. You can then decide if you should be changing your outlook or your friends. Continually associating with people who hold contrary opinions is fatiguing and an obstacle to success.

Friends who view everything negatively can be frustrating and contribute to stress-related symptoms.

Success can separate you from many friends, if you have a little success they can praise you, but if it is much more, it can make them feel uncomfortable.

If we wish our lives to have a purpose, we must prepare a plan which would be of value to us. Goal-setting, which is a skill in itself, can supply that value and is crucial in motivating us. Goals keep you on course, and together with a positive attitude create opportunities that will help you accomplish them. They will add a purpose to your life. Fully engaging in activities and challenging pursuits is necessary if we wish to enjoy a full life.

You need a plan to achieve any goal. If you have a goal in your life and have no specified plan for its achievement, it will probably never be more than an unfulfilled dream. Having a settled purpose, and being immersed in its expectation, will help eliminate stress and success will follow, as your mind produces positive energies when your perception of your goal is clear and intense. Consistent aims and a methodical approach are important and necessary in order to achieve your goals and turn your dreams into reality.

Much stress stems from fear of failure, although failures can be very productive in helping you achieve your goals. Very often, success comes disguised as failure. You can learn from the failure by analyzing its cause, and this can provide an opportunity to turn it into success. Failures have been known to be a blessing in disguise. Some of us have a failure-based personality, which in itself creates failure as often we get what we expect. It is ridiculous to believe that you will fail in exactly the same way a second time, this is extremely unlikely. Bad experiences can be used positively, as there is always some element to be learned to prevent future mistakes.

It may seem a paradox but failures have been known to be great motivators, as they can help you understand the basic problems. You cannot realistically expect that nothing can possibly go wrong, and you will succeed in everthing you do. Failure exposes our weaknesses and encourages us to face up to the consequences of these weaknesses. Very often, failure is needed as a reminder to count our blessings. It is the price we have to pay for enlightenment, and a reminder that there are other important values in our life, which are not dependent on financial success and which we take for granted when things go well. This realization can strike us very suddenly, and if any experience really teaches us anything, it is the experience of overcoming adversity.

Generally the things we worry about never happen, and we should, therefore, be able to bear our concerns without being overcome by them. Obstacles are eventually pushed aside and we successfully fulfil our purpose when we adopt a calm and patient conduct. Very often, unexpected circumstances change situations and our problems solve themselves. You can be flexible if you have a strong sense of purpose and an optimistic plan. It requires self-discipline, but the rewards are immense as you will be concentrating on what is happening in the present and with things you can comfortably do something about, and refusing to allow your mind to be dominated by fears.

It is of vital importance to recognize what is in your ability to control, and what is not, in order to overcome a common cause of stress. We must set achievable goals, which should be planned in stages, with sufficient time for each stage to be completed. It would be foolish to give priority to a goal which, although it may be important, is not at present within our capabilities. This could be depressing as it would be too big a demand on your time. It is always better to aim for short-term goals first which, when accomplished, will eventually lead us to our main objective.

A new approach to managing stress is to go about your tasks in a completely leisurely manner. By harnessing your pressures and cultivating a new skill you can achieve success without stress. And this will produce a confidence that will enable you to overcome many difficult situations unscathed. You will cease to think about problems on which no action can be taken at the moment, as you will be concentrating your total attention on the task at hand, while remaining relaxed without strain or effort.

It is wise sometimes to forget a problem for a while, to take a vacation from a seemingly insoluble worry. You are suspending judgement to a later date, when you can take a fresh look at the problem. Dismissing the problem for a few days, and then returning to re-think it over could be the best method of solving it.

We can change what we do, and how we do them, by positive re-thinking. Once we have acquired a mental discipline, we will learn to accept problems, even the serious ones, as mere challenges which we will have full confidence in overcoming. If we examine carefully any past experience which is relevant to our present situation, we may find our problems are being caused either by our wrong actions or inactions. Without problems, life would be boring and we would lose our ability to think. Having problems can help improve our minds, and we achieve a sense of satisfaction by overcoming them.

Our energies thrive on achievement, the more we achieve, the more encouraged we are to expend further energies into our plans. We will develop a sense of security, which is the basis of a successful life. We then know we are moving steadily in the right direction, exercising our talents and abilities to the full and experiencing a sense of freedom and self-realization.

THE NATURE OF MEN IS ALWAYS
THE SAME IT IS THEIR HABITS
THAT SEPARATE THEM.

CONFUCIUS

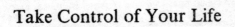
Take Control of Your Life

9

The circumstances we find ourselves in are the result of every decision we have made in our lives. Our personal experiences vary according to how we perceive them, and their importance is determined by our reaction to them. If these experiences do not interest us, we make nothing of them. Contemplative people have a genuine craving for a deeper and more satisfying meaning to their lives, whether they are struggling to subsist or attempting to avoid being prey to boredom.

Normally our minds are too ego-centred to broaden them by honest reflections and impersonal self-observations. There is an invisible and intuitive force within us all. If we wish to achieve control of ourselves, we must understand how to contact it. Only when we concentrate on honestly revealing the truth about ourselves, will we have found the instrument to do so. An undisciplined mind will inevitably resist the determination needed for achieving this contact.

Some of us are handicapped by making mountains out of molehills, and then worrying about the imaginary problems we ourselves have created. Taking control of your life means turning from a negative way of viewing things to a positive one, and inspiring yourself to take a deliberate turn in a chosen direction. Positiveness releases hidden energies; deprived of them, your mind is never brought under control. We may be squandering much of our energy by failing to awaken the power needed to create the life we want for ourselves, and thereby ignoring a more meaningful world of greater significance. Our minds hold undreamed of creativity, talents and abilities, which we are not generally conscious of possessing. The purpose of this book is to help you enjoy the fulfilment of this potential, utilizing your subconscious mind more fully, through its intuitive messages. Each message will succeed in producing others, and a deeper meaning to your existence will become clear.

We can accept responsibility for most situations

which affect us, either for better or worse. If we have control over our life, we are more likely to be better prepared for overcoming difficulties. We may feel that we have missed our intended purpose in our life, which can well be true. It can be difficult for some people to change from a mental restlessness, to a patiently creative way of behaving. It also may not be easy to sustain an ability to concentrate on goals, as your mind may protest against the unaccustomed new habits forced on it.

Success depends entirely on keeping your aims in view; it is unreasonable to expect success at the first attempt, and we should certainly not be discouraged by the fact we do not manage it. If we use a little more energy and determination, ultimately we shall succeed. In order to achieve success it is essential that we analyse that we are thinking and know ourselves more fully, by paying attention to the kind of thoughts which occupy our minds.

By deliberately subjecting ourselves to an honest self-analysis, rejecting any self-deception, we will be the beginning of a more humble and worthwhile way of living. The purpose is to open a door to our real self, thereby achieving an inner tranquillity. We have to understand who we are as we may seem to be several different people. We could discover we have achieved many merits to our credit, and thus avoid falling prey to self-criticism which would defeat our whole purpose.

Are we taking steps to fulfil ourselves and to devote our efforts to finding a purpose in our current life? Do we know who we really are and what makes us happy? Is it possible that we really did not want some of the things we sacrificed so much to obtain? If we feel a great lack, it may not be life itself which prevents us from reaping the benefits of an inner peace, but the interruptions we permit to clutter our path. We should not allow anything to distract us from having a positive vision of our realistic goals.

It is vital to maintain a perspective on all matters which can improve our circumstances, and we should harness our desires by avoiding distracting insignificant matters which overwhelm us. If necessary, we must accept our mistakes, making sure that they are not replicas of our previous ones. With a little concentration and a positive attitude you can maintain a control of your life, which will result in a new secure degree of freedom. **You will cease being tossed around by circumstances when you accept that your actions can control external events, and you will**

prove false the notion that your life is at the mercy of
Fate.

> EXCELLENCE IS NOT AN ACT,
> BUT A HABIT. WE ARE WHAT WE
> REPEATEDLY DO.
>
> ARISTOTLE